MOCKTAILS
PUNCHES & SHRUBS

MOCKTAILS
PUNCHES & SHRUBS

VIKAS KHANNA

CONTENTS

HERE'S TO HEALTH AND HAPPINESS

Whether served in crystal decanters or in antique silver teapots, artfully styled drinks provide the perfect prelude to an afternoon or evening of fine food, creating an atmosphere of warmth, conviviality, and hospitality. This dazzling collection of drinks, including some timeless classics and exciting modern recipes, will go a long way to creating a room full of happy and appreciative guests.

One of the most important aspects of anything we eat or drink is pleasure. We are bombarded with scents and flavours every day, and these experiences can be stored with surprising vividness for a very long time. We all have childhood memories of our ultimate comfort drinks: as kids, some of us woke up to the smell of coffee, while for others it was fruity, juicy morning drinks. For me it was warm milk scented with cardamom, sometimes garnished with almond slivers. I spent most of my childhood experiencing flavours and tastes of foods and drinks from around India. The nostalgia of smelling perfumed cardamom chai in a clay pot, and the kokum-flavoured coconut milk served before a lavish spread of south Indian delicacies, still lingers on. I also learned how to combine the woody flavour of cumin with the liquorice taste of star anise, or cool mint with lemony coriander, and I remember creating a thick jam in Kashmir using the sweet-tart flavours of cherries and combining them with the slightly liquorice flavour of fennel seeds.

Inspired, I embarked on a quest to collect and catalogue as many flavours and scents from foreign cultures as possible. A plethora of tasting experiences provided me with insights on what is mixable, edible, and, most importantly, what can stimulate and benefit us in a positive way. This collection of drinks is a fruition of all those experiences and insights. Ranging from herbal infusions to new combinations of teas and tantalizing elixirs and smoothies to shrubs and slushies, these drinks take little time to prepare, yet taste so good. Put your own spin on classic concoctions, mix and match garnishes and adornments, and stir up some modern fusion drinks using ingredients such as passion fruit, kumquats, and radishes; with a few of these simple preparations, you will have something new to bring to the table. These versatile recipes will also allow you to play with your imagination and create drinks for any occasion, while keeping the flavour and wholesome goodness of the ingredients intact.

So, get ready to serve up some good-spirited fun and dazzle your guests with your creativity. Hope you enjoy working with these recipes as much as I did creating them.

Cheers!

Vikas Khanne.

ESSENTIAL INGREDIENTS

While the recipes in this book include a wide variety of ingredients and exciting flavours, there are certain basic ingredients that you should keep handy so that you're always prepared.

Citrus fruits
Refreshing, tart, and acidic, citrus fruits such as lemons, limes, and oranges are key ingredients in many drinks. For the best flavour use fresh fruits, not the bottled juices you see in the store.

Fresh root ginger
Ginger root is the rhizome of the ginger plant, which is native to warmer parts of Asia. Despite its pungent, earthy, sweet-spice flavour, ginger is an incredibly versatile ingredient that pairs well with almonds, apricots, cinnamon, cranberry, honey, lemon, and salt, to name just a few. It also acts as a great counter-balance to greens such as kale, spinach, and parsley.

Grenadine
Both sweet and tart with a deep red colour, grenadine is a popular ingredient in drinks. It's traditionally made from pomegranates, however today some brands are made from just corn syrup and colouring. For the best flavour, check the ingredients on the bottle and make sure you're purchasing one made from real pomegranates.

Mint
Cool, clean, and refreshing, mint is a classic garnish in summer drinks. Use only fresh mint and use it as soon as possible. Discard any leaves that are wilted or brown as they will spoil the flavour and appearance of your drink.

Peppercorns
Pepper has different characteristics depending on its origin. Black peppercorns have a bold and biting taste, whereas white peppercorns have a sweetish afternote. Tellicherry, a variety of black pepper grown in Kerala, India, has the largest berries and is considered by many to be the best quality. Pepper adds a pungent flavour and warm aroma to drinks.

Pink peppercorns
The berries of the Brazilian pepper tree, pink peppercorns are pleasantly fruity, with a clear note of pine, but lack the heat of black pepper. Although resembling black peppercorns in both shape and taste, pink peppercorns are not

actually peppercorns at all, but a member of the cashew and mango family. The berry of a pink peppercorn has a brittle outer shell enclosing a hard seed.

Pomegranate
Considered a symbol of life in many cultures due to the scores of jewel-like seeds contained inside the tough skin, pomegranate is used extensively in Middle Eastern cuisine. It imparts an earthy, sweet and sour flavour into drinks. When buying pomegranates look for fruits with shiny, unblemished skins and avoid any that have soft patches. A fruit that is heavy for its size will yield the most juice.

Sea salt
Salt blocks bitter flavours and enhances sweet and sour flavours, which means in small quantities it can help to perfectly balance a drink. Think of the classic caramel and sea salt pairing and how the salt helps to bring out the rich flavours of the sweet caramel. The same principle can be applied when mixing drinks.

Soda water
Carbonated water is an integral mixer in many drinks, alcoholic and non-alcoholic alike, due to its neutral flavour that can be used with anything from fruit juice to shrubs. The fizziness can make a simple drink suddenly seem like a special indulgence. Always keep several bottles on hand so you never find yourself without a mixer.

Sugar
Just like sour, salty, and bitter, sweet is one of the recognised basic flavours of taste. For well-rounded food and drinks that don't seem overpowering, flavours should balance and complement one another. Sweetness acts as a counter-balance to sour, helps to minimize bitterness, and provides body to a drink. There are many different types of sugar available, from simple white caster to dark brown muscovado, all with their own special flavours and uses.

Vanilla extract
Vanilla is the bean-like fruit of a climbing orchid native to Central America and other tropical areas, such as Kerala in India. Vanilla extract is made by macerating the pods in alcohol. It has a sweet aroma and delicate taste and is commonly used to flavour desserts.

FRUITY FLAVOURS

WARM MANGO, PINEAPPLE, AND CHIA PUNCH

Serves **4** Takes **10 mins, plus chilling overnight**

Ingredients

2 tbsp chia seeds

240ml (8fl oz) mango pulp, or the flesh of 1 large mango, blended until smooth

240ml (8fl oz) pineapple juice

Method

1 Add the chia seeds to 120ml (4fl oz) of hot water and stir to disperse them evenly. Cover and refrigerate overnight.

2 Combine the mango pulp and pineapple juice in a saucepan and cook over a low heat until warm.

3 Pour the warmed juice into 4 glasses. Add a spoonful of soaked chia seeds to each glass and serve immediately.

ALTHOUGH ALL TROPICAL FRUITS BLEND WELL, IT IS THE MANGO AND PINEAPPLE FLAVOURS THAT TAKE CENTRE STAGE HERE; LOADED WITH VITAMIN C AND ANTIOXIDANTS, THESE TWO FRUITS MAKE A DELICIOUS AND UPLIFTING SUMMER DRINK. ADD SOME EXTRA CHIA SEEDS IF YOU WANT TO TURN THIS INTO A GREAT BREAKFAST DRINK.

KUMQUAT, PINEAPPLE, AND PAPRIKA DRINK

Serves **6** Takes **8 mins**

Ingredients

200g (7 oz) kumquats, deseeded and thinly sliced

60ml (2fl oz) pineapple juice

1 tbsp ginger juice

50g (1¾ oz) sugar, or to taste

soda water, chilled

1 tsp paprika

CHEF'S TIP

To make ginger juice, peel and finely grate fresh root ginger, then squeeze the grated ginger to release the juice.

Method

1 Gently muddle the kumquats, pineapple juice, ginger juice, and sugar with a wooden spoon until the kumquats give out their citrusy flavour and fragrance.

2 To serve, divide the mixture equally between 6 flute glasses, top up with soda water, and sprinkle a little paprika on top of each drink.

TANGY KUMQUATS CAN INSPIRE MANY A DRINK, ESPECIALLY WHEN THEIR SOFT, SWEET EDIBLE PEEL IS USED. HERE, THEIR FLAVOURS ARE EXTRACTED BY MUDDLING THEM WITH PINEAPPLE JUICE AND SUGAR TO CREATE A VELVETY SMOOTH TEXTURE.

PLUM PUNCH WITH CARDAMOM

Serves **4** Takes **8 mins, plus cooling**

Ingredients

450g (1lb) ripe plums, pitted

50g (1¾ oz) sugar

¼ tsp freshly ground cumin

6 cardamom pods, skin removed

¼ tsp pink salt

crushed ice, as required

Method

1 In a saucepan, bring 480ml (16fl oz) of water to the boil over a medium–high heat. Add the plums and cook for 3–4 minutes until they become soft and mushy. Strain and allow to cool.

2 Using a blender, blitz the cooked plums with the sugar, cumin, cardamom pods, salt, and crushed ice until smooth and fragrant.

3 Pour the drink into 4 glasses and serve immediately.

MAKING HOME-MADE PLUM PURÉE HELPS TO PRESERVE BOTH THE NATURAL GOODNESS OF THE PLUMS AND THEIR DEEP, DENSE COLOUR. ADDING CARDAMOM BRINGS OUT THE AROMATIC UNDERTONES OF THIS DRINK.

GRAPEFRUIT AND GUAVA SQUEEZE

Serves **4** Takes **5 mins, plus chilling**

Ingredients

960ml (1¾ pints) grapefruit juice

240ml (8fl oz) guava juice

juice of 1 lemon

pinch of rock salt

8–10 fresh basil leaves,
cut into chiffonaded strips,
to garnish

Method

1 Combine the grapefruit juice, guava juice, lemon juice, and salt in a large mixing bowl. Leave to chill for 2–3 hours in the fridge.

2 Pour into 4 glasses and serve garnished with the basil strips.

VIBRANT IN BOTH COLOUR AND TASTE, THIS ADDICTIVE, SMOOTH COMBINATION OF GUAVA AND GRAPEFRUIT MAKES AN INVIGORATING BEVERAGE ON A HOT SUMMER EVENING. THE SWEET TASTE OF GUAVA AND TANGY, ANTIOXIDANT-RICH GRAPEFRUIT JUICE COMPLEMENT EACH OTHER PERFECTLY.

MANGOSTEEN AND LYCHEE NECTAR

Serves **4** Takes **5 mins, plus chilling**

Ingredients

480ml (16fl oz) **mangosteen juice**

480ml (16fl oz) **lychee juice**

1 tbsp **lemon juice**

2 tbsp **sugar, or to taste**

beetroot microgreens or mint leaves, to garnish

CHEF'S TIP
If you can't get hold of mangosteen or lychee juice, you can make your own at home by blending the flesh of ripe fruit and diluting it with a little water.

Method

1 In a jug, combine the mangosteen juice, lychee juice, lemon juice, and sugar. Stir until mixed well.

2 Allow to chill in the fridge, then pour into 4 glasses. Garnish with beetroot microgreens or mint leaves and serve.

AS WELL AS BEING RICH IN MINERALS AND VITAMINS, THIS DRINK IS A PERFECT HARMONY OF EXOTIC FLAVOURS AND AROMAS. SWEETLY FRAGRANT MANGOSTEEN JUICE PAIRS EXCELLENTLY WITH LYCHEE JUICE TO MAKE A DELICIOUS SMOOTH TROPICAL DRINK.

CHERRY, CHERRY EVERYWHERE

Serves **4** Takes **5 mins, plus chilling**

Ingredients

24 cherries, pitted,
plus extra to garnish

480ml (16fl oz) cranberry juice

240ml (8fl oz) coconut cream

juice of 1 lime

a few drops of vanilla extract

Method

1 Using a blender, blitz the cherries, cranberry juice, coconut cream, lime juice, and vanilla extract together.

2 Allow to chill in the fridge, then garnish with the remaining cherries and serve.

THIS IS A TANGY, REFRESHING SMOOTHIE, ACCENTED WITH THE TASTE OF FRESH CHERRIES — AN ALL-TIME FLAVOUR ENHANCER. COCONUT CREAM ADDS A THICK CONSISTENCY TO THE SMOOTHIE AND GIVES IT A DELICIOUS TROPICAL TWIST.

BLOOD ORANGE AND TAMARIND AGUA FRESCA

Serves **4** Takes **20 mins, plus cooling and chilling**

Ingredients

720ml (1¼ pints) blood orange juice, or the juice of 8 blood oranges

1 tbsp tamarind paste

For the cinnamon molasses

3 tbsp brown sugar

3 tbsp molasses

1 tsp cinnamon powder

1 tbsp butter

CHEF'S TIP

The recipe makes 120ml (4fl oz) of cinnamon molasses, more than is required for the drink. Use the rest to flavour other beverages.

Method

1 To make the cinnamon molasses, combine the brown sugar, molasses, cinnamon powder, butter, and 120ml (4fl oz) of water in a saucepan over a medium–high heat. Bring the mixture to the boil, stirring continuously.

2 Remove from the heat and allow it to cool to room temperature. Store in the fridge in an airtight container.

3 Using a blender, blitz the blood orange juice, tamarind paste, and 120ml (4fl oz) of water with 2 tablespoons of the cinnamon molasses. Strain into a jug and refrigerate until chilled. Then pour into 4 glasses with ice and serve.

A VERITABLE COCKTAIL OF FLAVOURS, THIS COMBINATION OF CITRUSY BLOOD ORANGE AND THE SPICY SWEETNESS OF CINNAMON MOLASSES PERFECTLY BALANCES THE TARTNESS OF TAMARIND.

ORANGE "CIDER" WITH CLOVES

Serves **4** Takes **30 mins, plus cooling**

Ingredients

8 large oranges

240ml (8fl oz) cloudy apple juice

1 tsp cloves

4 tbsp sugar

Method

1 Preheat the oven to 80°C (175°F/Gas ½). Place the oranges on a tray and bake for 15 minutes.

2 Remove the oranges from the oven. Once they have cooled down, squeeze out their juice. Reserve the peel of one orange and grate it to obtain the zest.

3 In a saucepan, combine the orange juice, zest, apple juice, cloves, and sugar. Cook until the sugar dissolves and the juice absorbs the flavour of the cloves. Strain into 4 glasses and serve hot.

DURING WINTER, WHEN ORANGES ARE IN ABUNDANCE, I LIKE TO COMBINE APPLE JUICE WITH ORANGES FOR A DIFFERENT FLAVOUR. THIS IS ALSO A GREAT LIQUID FOR POACHING FRUITS TO CREATE FLAVOURFUL DESSERTS.

GREEN APPLE, CHILLI, AND CELERY DRINK

Serves **4** Takes **5 mins, plus chilling**

Ingredients

3 green apples, cored and coarsely chopped

1 celery stick

2 green chillies, or to taste, coarsely chopped

1 tbsp honey, or to taste

6 tbsp full-fat yogurt

3–4 drops vanilla extract

4–6 green olives, pitted

680g (1½lb) baby spinach

120ml (4fl oz) apple juice

pinch of salt

Method

1 Using a blender, blitz the apples, celery, green chillies, honey, yogurt, vanilla extract, olives, baby spinach, apple juice, and salt. Blend until smooth.

2 Refrigerate and allow to chill well, then divide equally between 4 glasses and serve.

GREEN APPLES GO WELL WITH HONEY AND VANILLA, CREATING A SWEET-TART MEDLEY OF FLAVOURS. GREEN CHILLIES ADD A SPICY KICK TO THE DRINK, WHILE THE OLIVES IMPART A NATURAL SALTINESS.

OATS AND APPLE BREAKFAST

Serves **4** Takes **10 mins**

Ingredients

7.5cm (3in) cinnamon stick

45g (1½ oz) rolled oats

For the apple sauce

1 red apple, peeled, cored, and chopped

1 tbsp sugar

Method

1 To make the apple sauce, combine the apple and sugar with 3 tablespoons of water in a saucepan over a medium heat. Cook for about 4–5 minutes, adding a little more water, if required. Remove from the heat and transfer to a bowl to cool a little. Using a blender, blitz the mixture until smooth.

2 Combine the cinnamon stick with 1 litre (1¾ pints) of water in a saucepan and bring to the boil. Then set aside.

3 Divide the oats equally between 4 glasses and spoon a tablespoon of apple sauce into each glass.

4 Strain the cinnamon-flavoured hot water over the oats, stir, and serve immediately.

I LOVE TO GIVE MY OWN TWIST TO A DISH; HERE, I HAVE REDEFINED A NUTRITIOUS, HEALTHY BREAKFAST. YOU CAN PURÉE THE OATS TO GIVE A SMOOTH CONSISTENCY, BUT PERSONALLY I LIKE THE COARSE TEXTURE.

COOL AND REFRESHING

LIME TO LEMONS

Serves **4** Takes **10 mins, plus cooling**

Ingredients

4 sprigs fresh rosemary

**l tbsp Sichuan peppercorns
(optional)**

120ml (4fl oz) honey

**pinch of fleur de sel
(if unavailable, use sea
salt flakes)**

juice of l lime

juice of l lemon

ice cubes, as required

**a few fresh blackberries,
to garnish**

Method

1 In a saucepan, boil 240ml (8fl oz) of water with the rosemary sprigs, Sichuan peppercorns (if using), honey, and fleur de sel. Cook until the mixture becomes thick and syrupy.

2 Remove from the heat and allow to cool. Strain and reserve.

3 In a jug, combine the rosemary syrup, lime juice, and lemon juice with 720ml (1¼ pints) of water and stir to mix well.

4 To serve, pour the drink over ice in 4 glasses and garnish with the fresh blackberries.

THE ENTICING AROMA AND TASTE OF THIS ROSEMARY-INFUSED SYRUP ARE A GREAT MATCH FOR TART LIME AND LEMON JUICES, WHILE TONGUE-TINGLING SZECHUAN PEPPERCORNS ADD A DELICATE COMPLEXITY TO THIS DRINK.

RASPBERRY LEMONADE

Serves **4** Takes **15 mins, plus cooling**

Ingredients

225g (8oz) fresh or frozen raspberries, plus 4–6 extra to garnish

4 tbsp sugar

1 tsp fennel seeds

juice of 2 lemons

chilled water, as required

Method

1 In a saucepan, combine the raspberries with the sugar, fennel seeds, and 240ml (8fl oz) of water and bring to the boil over a medium heat. Cook until the raspberries are pulpy.

2 Remove from the heat, set the mixture aside, and allow to cool to room temperature.

3 Using a blender, blitz the raspberry mixture to a smooth purée. Strain and mix in the lemon juice.

4 Add a tablespoon of the mixture to each of the 4 glasses and top up with chilled water. Garnish with the reserved raspberries and serve.

ALTHOUGH LEMONADE IS ONE OF THE MOST POPULAR BEVERAGES AROUND THE WORLD, AS CHEFS WE ARE ALWAYS LOOKING TO CREATE OUR OWN SIGNATURE VERSION OF IT. THE SWEET, LIQUORICE FLAVOUR OF FENNEL SEEDS GIVES THIS DRINK A FANTASTIC TWIST.

APRICOT, HONEY, AND LEMON DRINK

Serves **4** Takes **2 mins, plus chilling**

Ingredients

950ml (1¾ pints) apricot juice

2 tbsp honey

juice of 1 lemon

1 tsp ginger powder

Method

1 Combine the apricot juice, honey, lemon juice, and ginger powder in a jug and mix well.

2 Refrigerate until chilled, then pour into 4 glasses and serve.

APRICOT JUICE IMPARTS ITS SWEET AND DELIGHTFULLY MUSKY FLAVOUR TO THIS DRINK, WHILE THE GINGER POWDER ADDS A SPICY KICK.

RHUBARB AND HONEY DRINK

Serves **4** Takes **25 mins, plus cooling**

Ingredients

3 stalks rhubarb, finely chopped

5cm (2in) cinnamon stick

2 tbsp honey, or to taste

5cm (2in) fresh root ginger

chilled water, as required

CHEF'S TIP
If rhubarb is difficult to find, use 400g (14oz) strawberries, hulled and coarsely chopped, and the juice of 1 lemon to get the same flavour.

Method

1 In a saucepan, combine the chopped rhubarb with 360ml (12fl oz) of water and the cinnamon, honey, and root ginger. Bring to the boil over a medium–high heat.

2 Cook until the rhubarb is tender. Remove from the heat and allow to cool.

3 Using a blender, blitz the mixture to a purée. Strain the mixture to get a smooth concentrate.

4 To serve, add a tablespoon each of the rhubarb concentrate to 4 glasses and top up with chilled water. Stir and serve immediately.

FRESH RHUBARB PURÉE WITH A HINT OF ROOT GINGER IS THE PERFECT SPRINGTIME FLAVOUR. THIS DRINK IS A DELIGHTFUL BRUNCH FEATURE AT ALL MY TERRACE PARTIES IN THE SPRING.

LEMONGRASS AND COCONUT DRINK

Serves **4** Takes **15 mins, plus cooling and chilling**

Ingredients

200ml (7fl oz) coconut milk

240ml (8fl oz) coconut water

2 stalks lemongrass

2 pieces star anise

4 tbsp sugar, or as required

chilled water, as required

Method

1 In a large jug, combine the coconut milk and coconut water and stir to combine. Chill the mixture until needed.

2 In a saucepan, combine the lemongrass, star anise, and sugar with 240ml (8fl oz) of water. Cook until the sugar dissolves and the syrup is fragrant. Stir in the chilled coconut mixture and remove from the heat.

3 Cool the syrup to room temperature. Strain into 4 glasses and top up with chilled water. Stir and serve.

ADD A STALK OF LEMONGRASS TO EACH GLASS AS A STIRRER TO ENHANCE THE CITRUSY FLAVOUR OF THIS DRINK. YOU CAN MAKE THE FLAVOURED SYRUP IN LARGE VOLUMES AND STORE IT FOR LATER USE TO SWEETEN ICED TEAS AND OTHER COLD BEVERAGES.

SAFFRON AND CINNAMON PUNCH

Serves **4** Takes **10 mins, plus cooling**

Ingredients

5cm (2in) cinnamon stick

5cm (2in) fresh root ginger

100g (3½ oz) sugar

½ tsp saffron strands, plus extra to garnish

ice cubes, as required

chilled water, as required

Method

1 In a saucepan, combine the cinnamon stick, ginger, and sugar with 360ml (12fl oz) of water and bring to the boil over a medium heat.

2 Add the saffron when the syrup is slightly thick, and cook for another minute. Remove the syrup from the heat and allow to cool to room temperature. Strain the syrup into a jug.

3 Add a tablespoon each of the syrup to 4 glasses, add ice to each glass, and top up with the chilled water. Garnish with the reserved saffron strands and serve immediately.

A PERFECT SUMMER DRINK, THESE COOLING FLAVOURS ARE WELL COMPLEMENTED BY THE SOOTHING COLOUR. SIT THE CINNAMON STICK IN THE COOLING SYRUP TO ALLOW ITS AROMA TO STEEP AND REMOVE JUST BEFORE SERVING.

CUCUMBERADE

Serves **4** Takes **10 mins, plus cooling and chilling**

Ingredients

200g (7oz) sugar

1 large cucumber

juice of 2 lemons

pinch of salt

Method

1 Combine the sugar with 240ml (8fl oz) of water in a saucepan and cook over a low heat until the sugar dissolves.

2 Using a mandolin slicer or a very sharp thin knife, carefully slice the cucumber lengthwise into strips.

3 Place the cucumber strips in a large clean sterilized jar and pour the sugar syrup over them.

4 Add the lemon juice, 480ml (16fl oz) of water, and the salt. Stir and allow to cool. Cover and refrigerate overnight. Divide between 4 glasses and serve chilled.

THIS WONDERFUL TAKE ON LEMONADE WAS SHARED BY JYOTI AUNTY, WHOM I MET ON A COOKERY SHOW I WAS HOSTING. ADDING THE CUCUMBER GIVES AN INNOVATIVE TWIST TO TRADITIONAL LEMONADE.

SASSY PEACH KARAT

Serves **4** Takes **12 mins, plus cooling and chilling**

Ingredients

120ml (4fl oz) golden syrup

1 tsp saffron strands

480ml (16fl oz) peach nectar

240ml (8fl oz) cloudy apple juice

ice cubes, as required

Method

1 In a saucepan, bring 120ml (4fl oz) of water to the boil. Add the golden syrup and saffron and mix until the two are well combined.

2 Remove from the heat and allow the saffron syrup to cool. Strain, cover, and leave to chill in the fridge.

3 In a jug, combine the saffron syrup, peach nectar, and apple juice. Pour into 4 glasses containing ice cubes and serve.

THIS DRINK, MARKED BY PURITY AND A REFINED TASTE, COMBINES THE SWEET NECTAR OF PEACH AND APPLE JUICE INFUSED WITH THE WARM FLAVOUR OF SAFFRON.

OMBRÉ POMEGRANATE ELIXIR

Serves **4** Takes **12 mins, plus chilling**

Ingredients

480ml (16fl oz) orange juice

120ml (4fl oz) cranberry juice

2 tbsp ginger juice (see Chef's tip, p14)

100g (3½ oz) fresh blueberries, plus extra berries to garnish

240ml (8fl oz) pomegranate juice

4 tbsp sugar, or to taste

Method

1 In a jug, combine the orange, cranberry, and ginger juices and stir well. Cover and refrigerate until chilled.

2 Using a blender, blitz the blueberries with the pomegranate juice and sugar to a purée. Cover and chill in the fridge.

3 Pour the orange–cranberry–ginger juice mixture into 4 glasses. Top with the pomegranate–blueberry purée. Serve garnished with the reserved fresh blueberries.

CRAFTED WITH A MÉLANGE OF JUICES – RANGING FROM DARK, SWEET POMEGRANATE AND BLUEBERRY TO THE TANGY-TART MIX OF ORANGE AND CRANBERRY – THIS DELICIOUS BLEND, WITH ITS BEAUTIFUL HUES, SETS THE MOOD FOR A STYLISH EVENING.

CARROT, WHITE GRAPE, AND MINT DRINK

Serves **4** Takes **5 mins, plus chilling**

Ingredients

480ml (16fl oz) carrot juice

455g (1lb) fresh
white grapes

½ tsp ground cinnamon

1 tsp lemon zest

handful of fresh mint
leaves, to garnish

Method

1 Using a blender, blitz the carrot juice with the grapes, cinnamon powder, and lemon zest until smooth.

2 Refrigerate until chilled. Garnish with the mint leaves and serve.

CARROT JUICE AND WHITE GRAPES, COMBINED WITH CINNAMON, MAKE A REVITALIZING ANTIOXIDANT BASE, WHILE LEMON ZEST ADDS A BURST OF CITRUSY TOP NOTES AND FRESH MINT LEAVES GIVE A REFRESHING FINISH.

SPARKLE AND FIZZ

CHERRY AND PARSLEY SHERBET

Serves **4** Takes **12 mins, plus resting and chilling**

Ingredients

200g (7oz) sugar

200g (7oz) fresh cherries, pitted

4 sprigs fresh parsley

2 tbsp honey

juice of 1 lemon

soda water, as required

Method

1 Combine the sugar with 240ml (8fl oz) of water in a saucepan and cook over a low heat, stirring continuously until the sugar dissolves.

2 Remove from the heat and add the cherries and parsley. Transfer the syrup to a sterilized glass jar and leave to rest for 2–3 hours.

3 Pour the flavoured syrup into 4 glasses and add the honey and lemon juice. Top up with chilled soda water and serve chilled.

A GREAT DRINK TO BEAT THE HEAT, THIS IS FILLED WITH THE SWEET AND TART TASTES OF CHERRIES AND LEMON. ADDING FRESH PARSLEY BALANCES THEIR FLAVOURS. YOU CAN PREPARE THE FLAVOURED SYRUP AHEAD AND REFRIGERATE IT FOR UP TO A MONTH.

LEMON, LIME, AND JASMINE MIST

Serves **4** Takes **10 mins**

Ingredients

3 lemons, quartered

3 limes, quartered

a few drops of jasmine essence

65g (2oz) sugar

1 litre (1¾ pints) chilled water or soda water

Method

1 Squeeze the juice of the lemons and limes into a jug and add the leftover peels.

2 Add the jasmine essence and sugar to 60ml (2fl oz) of water in a saucepan and stir until the sugar dissolves. Add to the jug of lemon and lime juices.

3 Top up with chilled water or soda water and mix well. Pour into 4 glasses and serve immediately.

YOU CAN SERVE THIS DRINK WARM, ESPECIALLY DURING WINTER, OR ADD TWO TABLESPOONS OF TAMARIND PASTE TO CREATE ANOTHER VERSION OF THIS RECIPE; TAMARIND NOT ONLY ADDS A SWEET-SOUR FLAVOUR, IT ALSO LENDS THE DRINK A DISTINCTIVE BEIGE COLOUR.

FRESH TURMERIC, HONEY, AND GUAVA DRINK

Serves **4** Takes **5 mins, plus chilling**

Ingredients

480ml (16fl oz) guava juice, or the flesh of 6 guavas, blended until smooth

5cm (2in) fresh root turmeric, peeled and grated

2 tbsp honey

360ml (12fl oz) ginger ale, or as required

Method

1 Using a blender, blitz the guava juice, fresh turmeric, and honey.

2 Strain into a jug and allow to chill in the fridge. To serve, pour into 4 glasses and top up with ginger ale.

THE LIGHT, TROPICAL FLAVOUR OF GUAVA IS COMPLEMENTED BY THE GINGERY, PEPPERY TASTE OF FRESH TURMERIC, AND IS TOPPED OFF WITH CHILLED FIZZY GINGER ALE. KNOWN FOR ITS ANTISEPTIC QUALITIES, TURMERIC ALSO LENDS THE DRINK A WONDERFUL COLOUR AND AROMA.

ICE BLUEBERRIES WITH WHITE GRAPEFRUITADE

Serves **4** Takes **12 mins, plus freezing and chilling**

Ingredients

200g (7oz) fresh or frozen blueberries

200g (7oz) sugar

6–8 sprigs thyme

480ml (16fl oz) white grapefruit juice, or the juice of 2 white grapefruit

juice of 1 lime

Method

1 Place 3–4 blueberries in each section of an ice-cube tray, pour a little water over the berries, and freeze overnight. Store the cubes in an airtight container in the freezer.

2 In a saucepan, combine the sugar and 120ml (4fl oz) of water over a medium–high heat and bring to the boil, stirring continuously.

3 Remove from the heat and stir in the thyme sprigs. Store in an airtight container in the fridge.

4 Combine 2 tablespoons of the thyme syrup with the grapefruit and lime juice in a bowl. Pour into 4 glasses, add a few blueberry ice cubes to each glass, and serve chilled.

I LIKE TO MAKE SUGAR SYRUPS INFUSED WITH DIFFERENT HERBS, AS THEY ADD A GREAT DEPTH TO THE DRINKS THEY SWEETEN. HERE, THE WOODY AND EARTHY FLAVOURS OF THYME-INFUSED SYRUP PAIR WELL WITH THE REFRESHING TARTNESS OF WHITE GRAPEFRUIT JUICE.

ALMOND SYRUP MIST

Serves **4** Takes **15 mins, plus cooling and chilling**

Ingredients

200g (7oz) white sugar

1 tbsp almond extract

1 tsp ginger, peeled and grated

480ml (16fl oz) cranberry juice

soda water, as required

Method

1 In a saucepan, combine the sugar with 120ml (4fl oz) of water over a medium–high heat. Bring to the boil, stirring continuously.

2 Remove from the heat and allow to cool to room temperature.

3 Stir in the almond extract, then store the syrup in the fridge in an airtight container.

4 In a jug, combine the almond syrup, grated ginger, and the cranberry juice. Top up with soda water (or see below) and allow to chill in the fridge before serving.

THE SWEET, NUTTY FLAVOUR OF ALMOND BLENDS WELL WITH CRANBERRY AND SPICY GINGER, INFUSING THE DRINK WITH ITS WARM AROMA. WHENEVER I MAKE THIS DRINK, I LIKE TO SERVE THE SODA WATER SEPARATELY SO THAT PEOPLE CAN MIX IT ACCORDING TO THEIR TASTE.

STAR FRUIT FIZZ WITH AGAVE

Serves **4** Takes **8 mins, plus cooling and chilling**

Ingredients

100g (3½ oz) sugar

2 tbsp agave nectar

2 pieces star anise

1 tbsp fennel seeds

2 star fruit, coarsely chopped, plus one extra, thinly sliced, to garnish

soda water, as required

handful of fresh mint leaves, to garnish

CHEF'S TIP
If you can't find star fruit, you can substitute a ripe pineapple or two green apples.

Method

1 In a saucepan, bring 120ml (4fl oz) of water to the boil. Add the sugar, agave nectar, star anise, fennel seeds, and star fruit. Stirring constantly, cook for 1 minute or until the sugar dissolves.

2 Remove from the heat and allow to cool. Strain and leave the syrup in the fridge to chill.

3 In a jug, combine the syrup with the soda water and stir well. Serve chilled over ice, garnished with star fruit slices and mint leaves.

STAR FRUIT MAKES A PERFECT COMBINATION WITH FIZZY SODA WATER AND AGAVE NECTAR — A VEGAN ALTERNATIVE TO HONEY. AGAVE DISSOLVES QUICKLY, BRINGING A DELICATE, SWEET TASTE, WHILE THE FENNEL SEEDS ADD A LIQUORICE TASTE TO THIS DRINK.

SUPERFOOD BOOST

GREEN MACHINE

Serves **4** Takes **5 mins**

Ingredients

455g (1lb 1¾oz) fresh spinach leaves

100g (3½ oz) frozen peas, thawed

6–8 sprigs parsley

1 large green apple, diced

2 celery sticks

4 tsp sugar

Method

1 Use a blender to blitz the spinach, peas, parsley, green apple, celery, and 480ml (16fl oz) of water together until smooth.

2 Strain, mix in the sugar, and stir until the sugar dissolves completely. Serve immediately.

ONE OF THE MOST WHOLESOME DRINKS IN THIS BOOK, THE GREEN MACHINE GIVES THE BODY ENERGY TO KEEP IT GOING DURING THE DAY. THE CODE WORD FOR THIS JUICE IS "5 GS" BECAUSE OF THE FIVE GREEN INGREDIENTS USED IN IT.

RASPBERRY AND CHIA DRINK

Serves **4** Takes **20 mins**

Ingredients

200g (7oz) fresh raspberries

2 tbsp honey, or to taste

2 tsp ginger juice (see Chef's tip, p14)

½ tsp pink salt

chilled water or soda water, as required

4 tbsp chia seeds, soaked in 60ml (2fl oz) water

Method

1 In a saucepan, combine the raspberries with a little water and bring to the boil over a medium heat until the raspberries are pulpy.

2 Remove from the heat. Mix in the honey, ginger juice, and salt and allow to cool.

3 Using a blender, blitz the raspberry mixture to a smooth purée.

4 To serve, spoon a tablespoon each of the raspberry purée into 4 tall glasses. Top up with the water or soda water and add a tablespoon of soaked chia seeds to each glass. Stir and serve immediately.

USED UNREFINED IN ITS NATURAL STATE, PINK SALT ADDS AN EARTHY AROMA WITH SWEET-SALTY UNDERTONES TO THIS DRINK, WHILE THE RASPBERRIES LEND A DELICATE BLUSH, COMPLEMENTED BEAUTIFULLY BY THE FLOATING CHIA SEEDS.

GOJI BERRY SHAKERATTO

Serves **4** Takes **20 mins, plus chilling and resting**

Ingredients

100g (3½ oz) dried goji berries

2 tbsp honey

juice of 1 lemon

1 tsp ginger powder

For the rice milk

200g (7oz) cooked long-grain rice, cooled

pinch of salt

pinch of sugar

Method

1 To make the rice milk, use a blender to blitz all the ingredients with 960ml (1¾ pints) of water until smooth. Using a piece of muslin, strain the mixture and refrigerate until required (this homemade drink will keep in the fridge for up to 2 days).

2 Soak the goji berries in 120ml (4fl oz) of hot water and leave to rest for 10–15 minutes.

3 Using a blender, blitz the soaked goji berries, honey, lemon juice, ginger powder, and rice milk to a smooth purée. Pour into 4 glasses and serve chilled.

I FIRST HAD THIS DRINK DURING MY VISIT TO TIBET. THE SWEET AND SLIGHTLY TANGY FLAVOUR OF GOJI BERRIES ADDS A FRUITY — ALMOST CRANBERRY-FLAVOURED — RAISIN-LIKE TASTE TO THIS WONDERFUL DRINK, WHICH IS ENRICHED WITH THE GOODNESS OF LIGHT, REFRESHING RICE MILK.

BEETROOT AND CELERY JUICE WITH BLACK SALT

Serves **4** Takes **5 mins, plus chilling**

Ingredients

720ml (1¼ pints) beetroot juice

4 tender celery sticks

¼ tsp black salt

juice of 1 lemon

pinch of black cardamom seeds, ground to a powder

Method

1 Using a blender, blitz the beetroot juice, celery sticks, black salt, lemon juice, cardamom, and a little water together until smooth.

2 Strain and chill in the fridge. Pour into 4 glasses and serve.

THIS HIGHLY NUTRITIOUS DRINK PACKS IN THE FLAVOUR OF VIBRANT RUBY-RED BEETROOT JUICE INFUSED WITH THE MILDER-TASTE OF CELERY JUICE. I PARTICULARLY LIKE ADDING A LITTLE BLACK SALT TO MY DRINKS WHENEVER I CAN, FOR THE EARTHY PUNCH IT ADDS TO THE FLAVOURS.

SPINACH AND GINGER BOOSTER

Serves **4** Takes **5 mins, plus chilling**

Ingredients

**900g (2 lb) fresh
spinach leaves**

455g (1lb 1¾ oz) fresh kale

**25g (scant 1oz) fresh
parsley leaves**

**1 tsp matcha powder
(if unavailable, use green tea)**

**5cm (2in) fresh root
ginger, coarsely chopped**

Method

1 Using a blender, blitz the spinach, kale, parsley, matcha powder, and ginger with 360ml (12fl oz) of water until smooth.

2 Strain the liquid and refrigerate until chilled. Divide between 4 glasses and serve.

SPINACH, KALE, AND PARSLEY – A SUPERFOOD TRIO THAT MAKES A TASTY AS WELL AS NUTRITIOUS SMOOTHIE. THE SWEET-SPICY TASTE OF FRESH GINGER ENLIVENS THE DRINK AND BALANCES THE OTHER FLAVOURS.

BROCCOLI AND MINT WITH GARLIC SALT

Serves **6** Takes **70 mins, plus chilling**

Ingredients

I medium broccoli,
cut into florets

I small bunch fresh
spinach leaves

15g (½ oz) mint leaves

3 garlic cloves

240ml (8fl oz) orange juice

For the garlic salt

40g (I½ oz) garlic

75g (2½ oz) salt

Method

1 To make the garlic salt, use a blender to blitz the garlic and salt to a smooth paste. Spread out the mixture on a baking tray and bake for about I hour at 180°C (350°F/Gas 4), until crisp. Set aside.

2 In a saucepan, bring the broccoli florets to the boil in 720ml (1¼ pints) of water and cook until tender.

3 Using a blender, blitz the broccoli (with a little of its cooking water), spinach, mint leaves, garlic, and orange juice until smooth.

4 Strain the liquid and mix in the garlic salt. Refrigerate until chilled. Pour into 6 glasses and serve.

THIS COMBINATION OF BROCCOLI, SPINACH, AND MINT LEAVES MAKES A REFRESHING DRINK. THE GARLIC SALT DISSOLVES EASILY AND LENDS THE DRINK A WONDERFUL AROMA. YOU CAN ALSO SERVE IT HOT AS A NOURISHING SOUP.

AVOCADO, YOGURT, AND GREEN CHILLI DRINK

Serves **4** Takes **5 mins**

Ingredients

**2 large avocados,
pulp scooped out**

2 green chillies

¼ tsp sea salt

crushed ice, as required

For the vanilla yogurt

240ml (8fl oz) yogurt

½ tsp pure vanilla extract

Method

1 To make the vanilla yogurt, combine the yogurt with the vanilla extract in a bowl and mix well.

2 Using a blender, blitz the avocado pulp, green chillies, sea salt, crushed ice, and vanilla yogurt together until smooth.

3 Pour the mixture into 4 glasses, and serve.

VANILLA YOGURT IS ADDED FOR ITS FRAGRANCE AND SWEET CREAMINESS IN THIS DELICIOUSLY SATISFYING AVOCADO SMOOTHIE. ITS SWEETNESS IS PERFECTLY BALANCED BY THE SPICY SAVOURY TASTE OF THE SEA SALT AND GREEN CHILLIES.

ROCKING RADISH BOOSTER

Serves **4** Takes **5 mins**

Ingredients

**8–10 radishes,
coarsely chopped**

1 banana, coarsely chopped

2.5cm (1in) fresh root ginger

**480ml (16fl oz) vanilla yogurt
(see p70 for recipe)**

**beetroot microgreens, mint leaves,
or basil leaves, to garnish**

Method

1 Using a blender, blitz the radishes, banana, root ginger,
and vanilla yogurt until smooth and foamy.

2 Pour into 4 glasses, garnish with beetroot microgreens,
mint, or basil, and serve.

RADISH MAY SEEM LIKE AN UNUSUAL
INGREDIENT FOR A SMOOTHIE AT FIRST,
BUT IT MAKES FOR A DELICIOUS DETOXIFYING
DRINK FOR BREAKFAST, ADDING A PEPPERY
TASTE THAT IS BALANCED WELL BY THE
SWEETNESS OF THE BANANA.

FIG SMASH

Serves **4** Takes **5 mins, plus chilling**

Ingredients

240ml (8fl oz) fresh
sugar cane juice (if
unavailable, use
ready-made sugar
cane juice)

240ml (8fl oz) white
grape juice

8–10 dried figs

2 tbsp brown sugar,
or to taste

2–3 fresh figs, sliced
vertically, to garnish

Method

1 Using a blender, blitz the sugar cane juice, grape juice, dried figs, and sugar until smooth.

2 Strain into a jug and refrigerate until chilled. Serve garnished with fresh fig slices.

I LOVE THE TEXTURE OF FIGS AND THEIR SUBTLE, ADDICTIVE SWEETNESS. I PREFER MAKING THIS DRINK WITH FRESHLY SQUEEZED SUGAR CANE JUICE INSTEAD OF READY-MADE JUICE, ESPECIALLY IN SUMMER WHEN THIS HEARTY AND WHOLESOME DRINK IS MOST WELCOME.

TANGY SHRUBS

BEETROOT AND RHUBARB SHRUB

Serves **4** Takes **10 mins, plus chilling**

Ingredients

240ml (8fl oz) carrot juice

240ml (8fl oz) beetroot juice

2 stalks rhubarb, chopped, plus extra to garnish

2 tbsp honey

1 tbsp vinegar

3–4 tbsp sugar

1 tsp dried mint

chilled soda water, as required (optional)

Method

1 Using a blender, blitz the carrot juice, beetroot juice, rhubarb, honey, and vinegar until smooth.

2 Strain into a jug, cover, and refrigerate for a couple of hours.

3 Place the sugar and dried mint in a shallow dish and stir gently to combine the ingredients. Moisten the rims of 4 glasses with water and dip the rim of each glass into the sugar mixture to coat it.

4 Carefully pour the drink into the rimmed glasses. Top up with the soda water (if using). Garnish with rhubarb stalks and serve.

SHRUB, A FRUIT- AND VINEGAR-BASED DRINK, HAS ITS ROOTS IN 18TH-CENTURY ENGLAND, AND WAS CREATED AS A WAY OF PRESERVING FRUITS IN THE DAYS BEFORE REFRIGERATION. HERE, I HAVE COMBINED CARROT, BEETROOT, AND RHUBARB WITH A LITTLE VINEGAR TO CREATE A HEALTHY, REFRESHING DRINK.

GINGER-ORANGE SHRUB

Serves **4–6** Takes **5 mins, plus chilling**

Ingredients

2 oranges, preferably Navel oranges

5cm (2in) piece fresh ginger root, peeled and coarsely chopped

pinch of saffron threads, plus extra to garnish

200g (7oz) sugar

120ml (4fl oz) apple cider vinegar

chilled soda water, as required

ice cubes, as required

Method

1 Peel the oranges and gently remove most of the white pith. Transfer the orange segments to a large glass jar with a tight-fitting lid, add the ginger root, saffron threads, sugar, and vinegar, and muddle the ingredients until they are well combined and release their flavours.

2 Screw on the lid and shake the jar well. Using a piece of muslin, strain the mixture into a jug and refrigerate until chilled.

3 Top up with chilled soda water and serve over ice.

THE ACIDITY OF FRESHLY SQUEEZED ORANGE JUICE MAKES IT A PERFECT BASE FOR A REFRESHING SHRUB. HERE, I'VE COMBINED IT WITH ZINGY FRESH ROOT GINGER AND DELICATELY FLAVOURED SAFFRON.

RASPBERRY AND PEACH MEDLEY

Serves **4** Takes **20 mins, plus cooling and chilling**

Ingredients

200g (7oz) fresh raspberries

2 ripe peaches, stoned and coarsely chopped

200g (7oz) sugar

240ml (8fl oz) white wine vinegar

pinch of salt

chilled water or soda water, as required

ice cubes, as required

Method

1 Combine the raspberries, peaches, sugar, vinegar, and salt in a medium saucepan over a medium-high heat. Bring to the boil, stirring continuously until all the ingredients are well combined.

2 Remove from the heat and allow to cool to room temperature.

3 Strain the mixture into a clean glass jar, cover, and refrigerate. It will keep for up to three weeks in the fridge.

4 Top up with chilled water or soda water and serve over ice.

THIS BRIGHT SHRUB IS A CELEBRATION OF THE FLAVOURS OF FRESH FRUIT. TOP WITH SODA WATER AND HALVED RASPBERRIES FOR A STUNNING SUMMER DRINK.

ELDERFLOWER-MANGO SHRUB

Serves **4** Takes **5 mins, plus cooling and chilling**

Ingredients

200g (7oz) fresh or ready-made mango pulp

2 tbsp elderflower essence (if unavailable, use elderflower cordial)

l tsp cumin seeds, roasted and coarsely ground

200g (7oz) sugar

240ml (8oz) apple cider vinegar

chilled water or soda water, as required

ice cubes (optional)

Method

1 Combine the mango pulp, elderflower extract, cumin seeds, sugar, and vinegar in a medium saucepan over a medium-high heat. Bring to a boil, stirring continuously until all the ingredients are well combined.

2 Remove from heat and allow to cool to room temperature.

3 Strain the mixture into a clean glass jar, cover, and refrigerate. It will keep for up to three weeks in the fridge.

4 Top up with the water or soda water, add a few ice cubes to each glass if using, and serve chilled.

I'VE PAIRED RICHLY SWEET MANGO PULP AND FLORAL ELDERFLOWER WITH EARTHY CUMIN SEEDS AND TANGY APPLE CIDER VINEGAR FOR THIS FLAVOUR-PACKED SHRUB.

KIWI AND LIME SHRUB

Serves **4–6** Takes **5 mins, plus cooling and chilling**

Ingredients

200g (7oz) fresh kiwi purée

200g (7oz) sugar

4 tablespoons white vinegar

240ml (8fl oz) fresh lime juice

2 tbsp honey

chilled water, as required

crushed ice, as required

fresh mint leaves, to garnish

Method

1 Combine the kiwi purée, sugar, and vinegar with 480ml (8fl oz) of water in a saucepan over a medium heat and cook until the sugar dissolves.

2 Remove from heat and allow to cool to room temperature.

3 Stir in the lime juice and honey, transfer to a clean jar, cover, and refrigerate for at least 3 days before using.

4 Top up with chilled water and serve over crushed ice, garnished with the mint leaves.

THIS DELICATELY GREEN SHRUB MARRIES KIWI FRUIT WITH LIME JUICE AND FRESH MINT. IT'S A HEALTHY AND FLAVOURFUL ALTERNATIVE TO MINT-FLAVOURED COCKTAILS.

PLUM CHILLI SHRUB

Serves **4** Takes **5 mins, plus cooling and chilling**

Ingredients

6–8 plums, stoned and coarsely chopped

200g (7oz) sugar

240ml (8fl oz) white wine vinegar

1 tsp chilli powder

2 tbsp golden syrup

chilled ginger beer or water, as required

crushed ice, as required

10 fresh basil leaves, to garnish

Method

1 Combine the plums, sugar, vinegar, chilli powder, and golden syrup in a saucepan over a medium heat and cook until the sugar dissolves.

2 Remove from the heat and allow to cool to room temperature.

3 Strain the mixture, transfer to a clean jar, cover, and refrigerate for at least 3 days before using.

4 Top up with chilled ginger beer or water and serve over crushed ice, garnished with the basil leaves.

AROMATIC BASIL LEAVES AND FIERY CHILLI POWDER ADD LAYERS OF FLAVOUR TO THIS PLUM-BASED SHRUB. TOP IT UP WITH GINGER BEER FOR EXTRA HEAT AND FIZZ.

SMOOTHIES AND SLUSHIES

POOLSIDE WATERMELON SLUSHIE

Serves **4** Takes **5 mins, plus chilling**

Ingredients

720ml (1¼ pints) watermelon juice

240ml (8fl oz) soy yogurt (if unavailable, use regular yogurt)

2 tbsp caster sugar

a few drops of elderflower essence (if unavailable, use elderflower cordial)

handful of ice cubes

Method

1 Using a blender, blitz the watermelon juice, yogurt, sugar, elderflower essence, and ice cubes until slushy.

2 Refrigerate until chilled, then pour into 4 glasses and serve.

THE CREAMY TEXTURE OF WATERMELON JUICE IS PERFECTLY PAIRED WITH SWEET ELDERFLOWER ESSENCE TO MAKE THIS REJUVENATING SLUSH. I PREFER USING SOY YOGURT FOR ITS SUBTLE TASTE; IT IS ALSO A GREAT OPTION FOR THOSE WHO ARE VEGANS OR LACTOSE INTOLERANT.

ALOE VERA, WATERMELON, AND STRAWBERRY ICY

Serves **6** Takes **8 mins**

Ingredients

l fresh aloe vera leaf or 180ml (6fl oz) aloe vera juice

800g (1¾ lb) fresh watermelon flesh (with rind removed)

225g (8oz) fresh strawberries, sliced

l green chilli, chopped

2 tbsp sugar

pinch of salt

150g (5½ oz) crushed ice

Method

1 If using an aloe vera leaf, scoop out the gel from the leaf with a teaspoon.

2 Using a blender, blitz the gel with the watermelon, strawberries, green chilli, sugar, salt, and ice until smooth.

3 Divide equally between 6 glasses and serve immediately.

GELATINOUS ALOE VERA ADDS A DISTINCT TEXTURE TO THE CONTRASTING FLAVOURS OF SWEET WATERMELON, TANGY STRAWBERRY, AND SPICY CHILLI TO CREATE A GREAT-TASTING SUMMER DRINK. FOR A MILDER VERSION, SKIP THE CHILLI.

BLACKBERRY AND PINEAPPLE CRUSH

Serves **4** Takes **5 mins**

Ingredients

455g (1lb) fresh or frozen blackberries

2 tbsp honey

pinch of freshly ground black pepper

480ml (16fl oz) pineapple juice

juice of 1 lime

handful of crushed ice

Method

1 Using a blender, blitz the blackberries, honey, black pepper, pineapple juice, and lime juice together until smooth.

2 Divide the crushed ice between 4 glasses, then pour in the juice mixture and serve.

THE COMPLEMENTARY SWEET FLAVOURS OF BLACKBERRY AND PINEAPPLE ARE ENHANCED BY A HINT OF SPICE FROM THE BLACK PEPPER IN THIS REFRESHINGLY COOL SUMMER DRINK.

ZARZAMORA MIXER

Serves **4** Takes **5 mins, plus chilling**

Ingredients

200g (7oz) fresh or frozen blackberries

200g (7oz) fresh or frozen raspberries

200g (7oz) fresh or frozen blueberries

1 guava, deseeded and coarsely chopped

480ml (16fl oz) full-fat yogurt

2 tbsp caster sugar, or to taste

Method

1 Using a blender, blitz the blackberries, raspberries, blueberries, guava, yogurt, and sugar until smooth.

2 Refrigerate until chilled, then pour into 4 glasses and serve.

ZARZAMORA IS SPANISH FOR BLACKBERRY. IN SPAIN, IT IS COMMON TO MIX VARIOUS BERRIES TO MAKE AN ENERGIZING SMOOTHIE. HERE, I HAVE ADDED GUAVA, WHICH BRINGS A SWEET-TART FLAVOUR AND EXTRA DOSE OF ANTIOXIDANTS AND VITAMINS TO THIS DRINK.

BERRY AND YUZU HONEY BREEZE

Serves **4** Takes **5 mins, plus chilling**

Ingredients

360ml (12fl oz) yuzu juice
(if unavailable, use orange juice)

2 tbsp yuzu honey (if
unavailable, use orange
blossom honey)

240ml (8fl oz) beetroot juice

200g (7oz) mixed fresh or frozen
berries, coarsely chopped

coriander microgreens
or coriander leaves, to garnish

Method

1 Using a blender, blitz the yuzu juice, honey, beetroot juice, and mixed berries until smooth.

2 Refrigerate until chilled, then pour into 4 glasses, add a garnish of coriander microgreens to each glass, and serve.

THE SWEET-SOUR TASTE OF YUZU GOES VERY WELL WITH SWEET-TASTING MIXED BERRIES AND MELLOWS THE EARTHY FLAVOUR OF BEETROOT. GARNISHING WITH CORIANDER MICROGREENS GIVES A NICE FINISH TO THE DRINK. I LIKE TO MAKE THIS JUICE A DAY IN ADVANCE AND CHILL IT IN THE FRIDGE TO ENSURE THE FLAVOURS ARE WELL-BLENDED.

VANILLA AND YOGURT SLUSH WITH RASPBERRIES

Serves **4** Takes **15 mins, plus cooling**

Ingredients

1 stalk of lemongrass, crushed

720ml (1¼ pints) yogurt

4 tbsp honey

a few drops of vanilla extract

handful of crushed ice

226g (8oz) fresh raspberries, chilled

CHEF'S TIP
If fresh raspberries are unavailable, use frozen ones.

Method

1 Combine the lemongrass with 60ml (2fl oz) of water in a small saucepan over a medium–high heat. Bring to the boil, then remove from the heat and allow to cool.

2 Strain the lemongrass water into a bowl and add the yogurt, honey, vanilla extract, and ice. Using a blender, blitz the mixture well.

3 To serve, divide the raspberries equally between 4 glasses. Pour the slush over them and serve immediately.

THIS LEMONGRASS-INFUSED YOGURT DRINK IS PERFECT FOR ANY OCCASION. IF YOU WANT TO TURN IT INTO A SMOOTHIE, ADD A LITTLE BUTTERMILK OR MILK AND BLEND WELL.

COCONUT AND RASPBERRY SORBET

Serves **4** Takes **20 mins, plus chilling and freezing**

Ingredients

For the raspberry sorbet

200g (7oz) raspberries

50g (1¾ oz) sugar, or to taste

1 tbsp orange zest

For the coconut sorbet

240ml (8fl oz) coconut milk

50g (1¾ oz) sugar, or to taste

1 tbsp lemon zest

1 ripe banana

handful of fresh mint leaves, to garnish

Method

1 To make the raspberry sorbet, use a blender to blitz the ingredients together until smooth.

2 Refrigerate for about an hour, or until cooled. Transfer to an ice-cream maker and process according to the manufacturer's instructions. Place the sorbet in an airtight container and freeze, stirring occasionally, until it hardens.

3 To make the coconut sorbet, blend the ingredients together until smooth. Transfer to an airtight container and freeze overnight.

4 Take 4 glasses, place a scoop of coconut sorbet in each glass and top with a scoop of raspberry sorbet. Serve garnished with the mint leaves.

SWEET-SOUR RASPBERRY AND CREAMY COCONUT MAKE A DIVINE COMBINATION FOR SORBET. ONCE YOU GET THE HANG OF MAKING HOME-MADE SORBETS, WHY NOT CREATE YOUR OWN BLEND OF FLAVOURS.

STRAWBERRY AND CARDAMOM MEDLEY

Serves **6** Takes **10 mins, plus cooling and chilling**

Ingredients

455g (1lb) fresh strawberries, crushed

2 oolong teabags

2 tbsp sugar

4 cardamom pods, lightly crushed

Method

1 In a saucepan, combine the strawberries with 1.2 litres (2 pints) of water, the oolong teabags, sugar, and cardamom.

2 Bring to the boil over a medium–high heat and cook until the strawberries are mushy.

3 Remove from the heat and allow to cool. Discard the teabags.

4 Using a blender, blitz the mixture to a purée and strain. Refrigerate until chilled. Pour into 6 glasses and serve.

THIS IS A SIMPLE DRINK, WITH THE EARTHINESS OF OOLONG TEA LENDING A FAINT COLOUR AND PLEASANT AROMA TO THE FRUITY STRAWBERRIES.

FLORAL AND FRAGRANT

LAVENDER AND LIME SPARKLER

Serves **4** Takes **10 mins, plus cooling and chilling**

Ingredients

3 tbsp dried culinary lavender flowers

5cm (2in) cinnamon stick

6–8 cardamom pods, crushed

400g (14oz) sugar

juice of 3 limes

480ml (16fl oz) soda water, as required

ice cubes, as required

lemon slices, to garnish

Method

1 In a saucepan, combine 240ml (8fl oz) of water with the lavender flowers, cinnamon stick, and cardamom pods over a high heat and bring to the boil.

2 Stir in the sugar and cook until it is completely dissolved. Reduce the heat and simmer for 5 minutes. Remove from the heat and allow to cool. Strain and reserve.

3 In a jug, combine the lavender syrup with the lime juice, soda water, and ice and mix well.

4 Pour into 4 glasses and serve, garnished with lemon slices.

THE FLORAL NOTES OF LAVENDER HEIGHTEN THE TASTE OF THIS REFRESHING DRINK, ESPECIALLY WHEN COMBINED WITH RICH, WARM CINNAMON AND CARDAMOM. FOR AN ELEGANT FINISH, GARNISH EACH DRINK WITH A STEM OF LAVENDER.

ROSE SUNRISE REFRESHER

Serves **4** Takes **15 mins, plus cooling and chilling**

Ingredients

200g (7oz) sugar

8–10 drops of rose water

**25–30 rose petals,
plus extra to garnish**

a few drops of grenadine syrup

Method

1 In a saucepan, bring 120ml (4fl oz) of water to the boil and add the sugar, rose water, and rose petals. Stirring continuously, cook for about a minute or until the sugar dissolves.

2 Remove from the heat and allow the syrup to cool down. Strain and set aside.

3 In a jug, combine the sugar syrup with the grenadine syrup and a little water, as required. Refrigerate until chilled and then serve garnished with rose petals.

ANOTHER FAVOURITE OF MIDDLE EASTERN CUISINE, ROSE ADDS A CRISP SWEETNESS TO THIS DRINK WITHOUT OVERPOWERING IT. THE FRESHER THE ROSE PETALS, THE MORE FRAGRANT THE DRINK.

ELDERFLOWER, MANGO, AND GINGER DRINK

Serves **6** Takes **15 mins**

Ingredients

1 ripe Alphonso mango

1 tsp elderflower essence
(or elderflower cordial)

1 tbsp sugar

5cm (2in) fresh root
ginger, cut into juliennes

8–10 ice cubes

Method

1 Using a melon baller, scoop out little mango globes and set aside.

2 In a jug, combine 960ml (1¾ pints) of water with the elderflower essence and sugar. Stir until the sugar dissolves.

3 Spoon a few mango scoops and ginger juliennes into 6 glasses and add a few ice cubes to each.

4 Top up with the elderflower water and serve immediately.

THIS MANGO–GINGER COMBINATION WORKS BEAUTIFULLY WITH ELDERFLOWER ESSENCE. FOR VARIETY, ADD A CUP OF CRANBERRY JUICE TO BRING A LITTLE ACIDITY AND A LIGHT PINK FLUSH TO THE DRINK.

GRENADINE SPRITZER

Serves **4** Takes **15 mins, plus resting and chilling**

Ingredients

4 tbsp sugar

2.5cm (1in) cinnamon stick

4 dried rosebuds

1 star anise

480ml (16fl oz) pear juice

480ml (16fl oz) white grape juice

a few drops of grenadine syrup

100g (3½ oz) raisins, soaked in 120ml (4fl oz) warm water

240ml (8fl oz) soda water

edible pansies, to garnish (optional)

Method

1 In a saucepan, bring 120ml (4fl oz) of water to the boil. Add the sugar, cinnamon stick, rosebuds, and star anise. Cook, stirring constantly, for about 1 minute until the sugar dissolves.

2 Remove from the heat, cover, and leave to rest until all the flavours have steeped. Strain and reserve.

3 In a jug, combine the pear juice, white grape juice, and grenadine with the flavoured sugar syrup. Refrigerate until chilled.

4 Divide the raisins between 4 glasses and fill half of each glass with the juice mixture. Top up with soda water and serve garnished with edible pansies (if using).

THE SWEET PEAR AND GRAPEFRUIT JUICES OF THIS REFRESHING DRINK ARE INFUSED WITH FLORAL NOTES OF ROSEBUDS AND AROMATIC STAR ANISE, WHILE THE ADDITION OF SWEET-TART GRENADINE AND SPARKLING SODA WATER ADD THE PERFECT FINISHING TOUCHES.

HIBISCUS–GINGER ON THE ROCKS

Serves **4** Takes **25 mins, plus chilling**

Ingredients

45g (1½ oz) dried hibiscus, or rosehip, flowers

4 cloves

4 tsp brown sugar

4 tsp green tea leaves

2 tsp fresh orange zest

5cm (2in) fresh root ginger, finely grated

ice cubes, as required

Method

1 In a saucepan, combine the hibiscus flowers, cloves, and brown sugar with 1 litre (1¾ pints) of water and bring to the boil over a medium heat.

2 Boil for 4–5 minutes until the sugar dissolves and the mixture absorbs all the colours and flavours.

3 Add the tea leaves, orange zest, and ginger. Remove from the heat and allow the tea to cool. Strain and refrigerate until chilled.

4 Pour the chilled tea into 4 glasses and serve over ice cubes.

HIBISCUS HAS A RICH COLOUR AND A VERY SUBTLE, EARTHY FLAVOUR. HERE, I HAVE PAIRED IT WITH GINGER, WHICH ADDS A SPICY ZING TO THE DRINK AND HELPS ELEVATE THE DELICATE TASTE OF HIBISCUS.

SUGAR AND SPICE

CINDERELLA'S CHOCOLATE

Serves **4** Takes **10 mins**

Ingredients

200g (7oz) dark chocolate chips

120ml (4fl oz) fresh orange juice

240ml (8fl oz) almond milk

4–6 drops orange extract

2 tbsp molasses (or golden syrup if unavailable), or to taste

Method

1 Melt the chocolate chips in a heatproof bowl over a pan of simmering water.

2 Using a blender, blitz the orange juice, almond milk, orange extract, and molasses. Add the melted chocolate and blend again.

3 Pour the drink into 4 glasses and serve immediately.

THIS DRINK IS DEDICATED TO MY NIECE, MY LITTLE CINDERELLA, WHO LOVES IT FOR ITS PERFECT BALANCE OF FLORAL TONES AND CARAMELIZED SCENTS. ENJOY THIS DRINK OF CONTRASTING FLAVOURS HOT OR COLD.

STAR ANISE COFFEE

Serves **4** Takes **10 mins**

Ingredients

5cm (2in) cinnamon stick, broken, plus extra to garnish

6–8 cardamom pods

4 star anise

300g (10oz) coffee beans or ground coffee

milk, to taste

sugar, to taste (optional)

Method

1 In a coffee grinder, blitz the cinnamon stick, cardamom pods, star anise, and coffee beans. Brew the mixture in a filter coffee maker, using a paper filter. If you do not have a coffee grinder or filter coffee maker, brew ground coffee in a cafetière.

2 Pour the coffee into 4 cups, and add milk and sugar (if using). Place a cinnamon stick in each cup, and serve hot.

THE AROMA AND FLAVOUR OF COFFEE INFUSED WITH SPICY STAR ANISE IS INCOMPARABLE. THE CLASSIC COMBINATION OF CINNAMON AND CARDAMOM ADDED TO THIS FRESHLY GROUND COFFEE TURNS IT INTO A WARM AND COMFORTING DRINK TO WAKE UP TO.

SOY MILK COFFEE WITH GOLDEN SYRUP AND MINT

Serves **6** Takes **5 mins, plus chilling**

Ingredients

4 tbsp instant espresso coffee powder

480ml (16fl oz) soy milk

a few drops peppermint extract

3 tbsp golden syrup, or to taste

Method

1 Dissolve the instant coffee powder in 2 tablespoons of warm water.

2 In a jug, combine the diluted coffee powder, soy milk, mint extract, and golden syrup. Refrigerate until chilled, then pour into 6 shot glasses and serve.

ESPRESSO COFFEE GIVES THESE SHOTS A DARK, CONCENTRATED FLAVOUR. SOY MILK IS A GOOD ALTERNATIVE TO REGULAR MILK, ESPECIALLY FOR PEOPLE WHO ARE LACTOSE INTOLERANT. MINT ADDS ITS EVER-COOLING GOODNESS, WHILE GOLDEN SYRUP LENDS A THICK CONSISTENCY AND RICH SWEETNESS.

TRIPLE C DRINK

Serves **4** Takes **15 mins, plus cooling**

Ingredients

450g (1lb) fresh or frozen cherries, stoned

50g (1¾ oz) sugar

225g (8oz) dark chocolate chips

½ tsp ground cinnamon

960ml (1¾ pints) full-fat milk

Method

1 In a small saucepan, combine the stoned cherries with the sugar and 240ml (8fl oz) of water over a medium heat. Bring to the boil and cook until the cherries are mushy. Remove the cherry mixture from the heat and set aside to cool.

2 In another saucepan, combine the chocolate chips and ground cinnamon with the milk and heat over a medium heat, stirring continuously until the chocolate melts and combines with the milk. Remove from the heat and allow to cool to room temperature.

3 Using a blender, blitz the cooled cherry syrup with the chocolate–cinnamon milk until smooth. Strain the milk and heat until just hot but not simmering. Pour into 4 cups or glasses and serve immediately.

CINNAMON IS A CLASSIC COMPANION TO HOT CHOCOLATE, WHILE CHERRIES ADD A TINGE OF SOURNESS TO BALANCE THE BITTERSWEET TASTE OF THE CHOCOLATE.

CARAMEL INDULGENCE

Serves **4** Takes **15 mins**

Ingredients

480ml (16fl oz) Greek yogurt

1 tsp ground cardamom seeds

240ml (8fl oz) blood orange juice, or the juice of 5 blood oranges

1 tbsp maple syrup

75g (2½ oz) crushed ice

For the caramel

50g (1¾ oz) light brown sugar

50g (1¾ oz) dark brown sugar

4 tbsp unsalted butter

60ml (2fl oz) double cream

pinch of salt

½ tsp pure vanilla extract

Method

1 To make the caramel, combine the two kinds of sugar, butter, and double cream in a saucepan over a medium–high heat. Bring the mixture to the boil.

2 Stirring continuously, cook until the butter melts and the mixture is smooth. Reduce to a simmer and cook for another 5 minutes, stirring occasionally. Stir in the salt and vanilla extract. Set aside.

3 Using a blender, blitz the yogurt, cardamom seeds, blood orange juice, maple syrup, and crushed ice.

4 Divide the mixture between 4 glasses, drizzle a little caramel on top of each drink, and serve.

GREEK YOGURT GIVES THIS DRINK A RICH, SMOOTH TEXTURE, ALMOST LIKE A SILKY MILKSHAKE. INFUSED WITH THE HEADY FLAVOURS OF SWEET MAPLE AND BLOOD ORANGE, AND SPICED WITH CARDAMOM, IT BECOMES EVEN MORE MEMORABLE WHEN DRIZZLED WITH LUSCIOUS CARAMEL.

GRAPEFRUIT AND LEMON JUICE WITH CHILLI

Serves **6** Takes **10 mins, plus chilling**

Ingredients

960ml (1¾ pints) fresh or canned grapefruit juice

2 medium lemons, halved

2 tsp red chilli powder

Method

1 Pour the grapefruit juice into a jug, squeeze in the juice from the lemons, and also add the halved lemon peels. Add the chilli powder and 240ml (8fl oz) of water and stir to mix well.

2 Cover the jug and refrigerate overnight, allowing the flavours to steep and the essential oils from the lemon peel to absorb into the juice. Just before serving, strain and divide between 6 glasses.

ADDING CHILLI POWDER TO THIS DRINK BINDS THE SWEET-SOUR-BITTER FLAVOURS OF GRAPEFRUIT JUICE AND THE ACIDITY OF THE LEMONS TOGETHER.

POMEGRANATE LASSI WITH CHILLI POWDER

Serves **6** Takes **10 mins**

Ingredients

480ml (16fl oz) pomegranate juice

750ml (1¼ pints) yogurt

2 tbsp honey, or to taste

200g (7oz) crushed ice

2 tsp red chilli powder, to garnish

Method

1 Using a blender, blitz the pomegranate juice with the yogurt, honey, and crushed ice until smooth.

2 Pour the liquid into 6 glasses and sprinkle a little chilli powder on top of each. Serve immediately.

WHILE THE CHILLI POWDER HELPS TO BALANCE THE SOURNESS FROM THE POMEGRANATE AND YOGURT IN THIS DRINK, CINNAMON, FENNEL SEEDS, OR EVEN FRESH MINT LEAVES WOULD WORK VERY WELL AS ALTERNATIVE GARNISHES.

JADE MOUNTAIN

Serves **4** Takes **20 mins, plus cooling and chilling**

Ingredients

4 small Habanero chillies

4 tbsp honey

pinch of nutmeg powder

450g (1lb) dandelion leaves (if unavailable, use watercress)

450g (1lb) rocket leaves

240ml (8fl oz) pineapple juice

CHEF'S TIP

If Habanero chillies are unavailable, use red chillies mixed with jalapeños to create the same taste.

Method

1 In a saucepan, combine the Habanero chillies with the honey, nutmeg powder, and 120ml (4fl oz) of water over a medium heat. Cook until the mixture becomes thick. Remove from the heat and set aside to cool.

2 Using a blender, blitz the Habanero mixture, dandelion leaves, rocket, pineapple juice, and 120ml (4fl oz) of water until smooth.

3 Strain and refrigerate until chilled. Pour the mixture into 4 glasses and serve immediately.

THE SPICINESS OF HABANERO CHILLIES COMBINED HERE WITH THE SWEETNESS OF HONEY AND PINEAPPLE JUICE AND SLIGHT BITTERNESS FROM ROCKET IS ABSOLUTELY SENSATIONAL. FOR VARIETY, USE A COMBINATION OF PINEAPPLE AND CRANBERRY JUICES TO ADD A LITTLE TARTNESS.

PEARL SHOTS

Serves **4** Takes **30 mins, plus chilling**

Ingredients

5 tsp caster sugar

80ml (2¾fl oz) tapioca (also known as tapioca pearls)

240ml (8fl oz) acai juice (if unavailable, use cranberry juice)

480ml (16fl oz) rice milk (see p65 for recipe)

75g (2½ oz) ice cubes

Method

1 In a small saucepan, bring 480ml (16fl oz) of water to the boil. Stir in 1 teaspoon of the sugar, and cook over a medium heat until the sugar has dissolved.

2 Add the tapioca and cook for about 20 minutes, or until cooked through. Add more water if required.

3 Rinse, drain, and refrigerate the tapioca until chilled.

4 Mix the acai juice, rice milk, and the remaining sugar in a cocktail shaker. Add the ice cubes and shake until well combined.

5 Pour into 4 shot glasses, top with the chilled tapioca, and serve.

EVERY TIME I PASS THE BUBBLE TEA SHOPS IN NEW YORK'S KOREATOWN, I FEEL INSPIRED TO TRY MY OWN. I ESPECIALLY LIKE THE RICH CHOCOLATEY BERRY FLAVOUR OF ACAI JUICE MIXED WITH RICE MILK.

HAZELNUT LAKEHOUSE

Serves **4** Takes **20 mins**

Ingredients

300g (10oz) light brown sugar

110g (3¾oz) unsalted butter

60ml (2fl oz) evaporated milk

1 tsp vanilla extract

pinch of salt

2 bananas, diced

2 tbsp hazelnut syrup

450g (1lb) hazelnut ice cream (if unavailable, use vanilla ice cream)

Method

1 In a saucepan, combine the sugar, butter, milk, vanilla extract, salt, and bananas over a medium heat. Stirring continuously, cook until the caramel mixture thickens to the desired consistency.

2 Remove from the heat and separate the caramelized banana pieces into a bowl. Reserve the remaining caramel sauce.

3 Using a blender, blitz the banana pieces, hazelnut syrup, and hazelnut ice cream together until smooth.

4 Pour the mixture into 4 glasses. Drizzle the caramel generously over the top of each glass and serve.

THE CREAMINESS OF SWEET BANANAS CREATES AN INTOXICATING FLAVOUR WHEN COMBINED WITH CARAMEL, WHILE THE HAZELNUT SYRUP AND ICE CREAM TURN THIS INTO A MOUTH-WATERING DRINK.

SPICE-INFUSED CREAMY EGGNOG WITH BASIL SEEDS

Serves **4** Takes **12 mins**

Ingredients

2 eggs, separated

pinch of nutmeg powder

65g (2oz) sugar

960ml (1¾ pints) full-fat milk

240ml (8fl oz) double cream

1 tsp basil seeds (soaked in
2 tbsp water for 1 hour),
to garnish

Method

1 In a mixing bowl, beat the egg yolks with the nutmeg until light and fluffy.

2 Stir in the sugar, milk, and double cream until well mixed. Beat the egg whites until light and fluffy and add them to the mixture.

3 Pour into 4 glasses, top each with ½ teaspoon of the soaked basil seeds, and serve immediately.

NUTMEG IMBUES THIS CLASSIC HOLIDAY DRINK WITH A SEDUCTIVE AROMA. MAKE SURE YOU USE GOOD-QUALITY EGGS, AS THEY ARE USED RAW IN THIS DRINK.

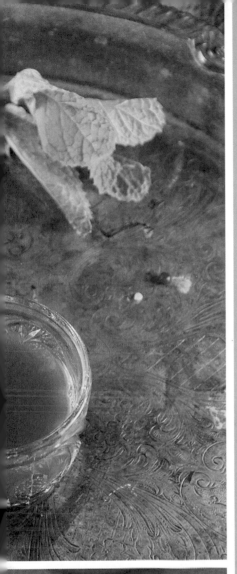

TIME
FOR TEA

LEBANESE ROSE TEA

Serves **4** Takes **15 mins, plus cooling**

Ingredients

4 teabags of strong tea

4 tsp demerara sugar

4–6 dried rosebuds

4 tsp pinenuts, lightly roasted

ice cubes, as required

For the pomegranate molasses

240ml (8fl oz) pomegranate juice

2 tbsp sugar

1 tbsp lemon juice

Method

1 To make the pomegranate molasses, combine the pomegranate juice, sugar, and lemon in a saucepan. Cook over a low heat until the mixture is reduced to a quarter of its quantity.

2 In a saucepan, combine the pomegranate molasses, tea bags, sugar, dried rosebuds, and pinenuts with 750ml (1¼ pints) of water and bring the mixture to the boil.

3 Remove from the heat after 2 minutes and allow the rosebud-infused tea to cool to room temperature.

4 Strain the mixture into 4 glasses. Add some ice cubes and serve.

CONSIDERED A SYMBOL OF LIFE, POMEGRANATE IS USED EXTENSIVELY IN MIDDLE EASTERN CUISINE. FOR AN EARTHY, SOUR FLAVOUR, USE POMEGRANATE JUICE INSTEAD OF THE POMEGRANATE MOLASSES.

PINK PEPPERCORN TEA

Serves **4** Takes **8 mins, plus cooling**

Ingredients

1 tbsp pink peppercorns, lightly crushed

100g (3½ oz) sugar

4 tsp Darjeeling tea leaves

8 sprigs fresh mint leaves

Method

1 In a saucepan, combine the peppercorns with the sugar and 120ml (4fl oz) of water and bring to the boil over a medium heat. Reduce the heat and simmer for 5–7 minutes. Remove from the heat and allow to cool.

2 Strain the mixture into another saucepan, add 960ml (1¾ pints) of water, and bring to the boil.

3 Add the Darjeeling tea leaves and mint leaves, brew for 1 minute, then remove from the heat.

4 Strain the tea into 4 cups and serve immediately.

THE BEST WAY TO EXTRACT THE SUBTLE PEPPERY YET FRUITY TASTE OF PINK PEPPERCORNS IS BY SLOWLY COOKING THEM IN WATER AND THEN COOLING THEM. I LOVE ADDING WHOLE SPRIGS OF MINT, AS THEY INFUSE THE TEA WITH A FRESH, WARM AROMA AND COOL AFTERTASTE.

SAFFRON AND ROSE TEA

Serves **6** Takes **12 mins**

Ingredients

½ tsp saffron strands,
plus extra to garnish

45g (1½ oz) pink rose petals,
plus extra to garnish

4 pieces of star anise,
plus extra to garnish

4 cardamom pods,
lightly crushed

4 tsp honey

2 tsp lemon juice

Method

1 In a saucepan, combine the saffron strands, rose petals, star anise, and cardamom pods with 1.2 litres (2 pints) of water and cook over a medium–high heat. Bring to the boil, then remove from the heat.

2 Strain into 6 glasses. Stir 1 teaspoon of honey and ½ teaspoon of lemon juice into each glass.

3 Garnish with a few saffron strands, rose petals, and star anise and serve while hot.

A CLASSIC COMBINATION, SAFFRON AND ROSE SYMBOLIZE FESTIVITIES AND CELEBRATIONS. THIS WARM, COMFORTING TEA IS SURE TO BECOME THE HIGHLIGHT OF YOUR NEXT WINTER PARTY.

GUJARATI LEMONGRASS TEA

Serves **4** Takes **8 mins**

Ingredients

4 tsp sugar

2 stalks lemongrass

1 tsp ginger powder

4 black teabags

240ml (8fl oz) skimmed milk

Method

1 In a saucepan, combine 750ml (1¼ pints) of water with the sugar, lemongrass, and ginger powder. Bring the mixture to a rapid boil over a medium heat.

2 Add the teabags and milk and let the mixture simmer for 1 minute. Remove from the heat, cover, and set aside for 2 minutes to allow the flavours to steep.

3 Discard the teabags. Strain into 4 teacups and serve immediately.

THE EARTHY, SWEET-SPICY TASTE OF GINGER POWDER COMBINES WITH THE CITRUSY FLAVOUR OF LEMONGRASS TO MAKE THIS REFRESHING DRINK, WHICH IS PERFECT FOR ANY TIME OF THE YEAR.

MELON AND BASIL BUBBLE TEA

Serves **4** Takes **30 mins, plus chilling**

Ingredients

5 tsp caster sugar

60g (2oz) tapioca, also known as pearl tapioca

450g (1lb) fresh melon

8–10 fresh basil leaves

240ml (8fl oz) brewed black tea

120ml (4fl oz) milk, or to taste

small handful of ice cubes

Method

1 In a saucepan, bring 480ml (16fl oz) of water to the boil on a high heat. Stir in 1 teaspoon of the sugar until it dissolves.

2 Add the tapioca and cook for 20 minutes, or until tender. Add more water if required. Rinse, drain, and refrigerate until chilled.

3 Using a blender, blitz the melon and basil leaves on a high speed to a smooth purée. Add a little water, if required.

4 Combine the melon–basil purée, the remaining sugar, tea, and milk in a cocktail shaker. Add ice cubes and shake until chilled.

5 Pour into 4 glasses, add equal amounts of the cooked tapioca to each glass, and serve.

THIS IS A MEMORABLE DRINK, WITH A UNIQUE GUM-LIKE TEXTURE. YOU CAN CREATE YOUR OWN VERSION OF BUBBLE TEA BY REPLACING MELON WITH ANOTHER FRUIT.

STAR ANISE AND MINT ICED TEA

Serves **4** Takes **25 mins, plus cooling**

Ingredients

50g (1¾ oz) sugar

4 star anise

2 tbsp green tea leaves

ice cubes, as required

handful of fresh mint leaves, to garnish

Method

1 In a saucepan, combine the sugar and star anise with 60ml (2fl oz) of water over a medium heat and bring to the boil.

2 Cook until the mixture thickens, remove from the heat, and allow to cool completely. Strain the syrup into a bowl and set aside.

3 In another saucepan, heat 1.2 litres (2 pints) of water until just hot but not simmering. Add the tea leaves and remove from the heat. Set aside and leave to cool to room temperature.

4 Strain the tea into a jug and stir in the star anise syrup. Add ice cubes to 4 glasses and pour the tea over them. Garnish with mint leaves and serve immediately.

THE REFRESHING FLAVOUR OF MINT IS OFTEN USED TO CREATE COOLING, SUMMERY DRINKS. HERE, IT IS COMBINED WITH THE LIQUORICE TASTE OF STAR ANISE TO CREATE A MEMORABLE DRINK.

CINNAMON AND LEMON COMFORT TEA

Serves **4** Takes **5 mins**

Ingredients

4 x 2.5cm (1in) cinnamon sticks

8 chamomile flowers

1 litre (1¾ pints) hot water

2 tsp honey

1 lemon, quartered

Method

1 Add a cinnamon stick, 2 chamomile flowers, and some of the hot water to each of the 4 cups.

2 Add ½ tsp honey and squeeze in a lemon quarter to each cup. Serve immediately.

CINNAMON IS THE SPICE MOST COMMONLY USED DURING FESTIVALS AROUND THE WORLD. THIS SOOTHING, ANY-TIME-OF-THE-DAY TEA CELEBRATES THE FESTIVE NATURE OF THE SPICE ALONGSIDE THE FLORAL NOTES OF SOOTHING CHAMOMILE.

CHINESE FIVE-SPICE CHAI

Serves **4** Takes **15 mins, plus cooling**

Ingredients

1 tbsp cloves

1 tbsp fennel seeds

1 tbsp black peppercorns

6–8 star anise

5cm (2in) cinnamon stick

4 tsp orange pekoe tea leaves

Method

1 In a small pan, lightly dry-roast the cloves, fennel seeds, peppercorns, star anise, and cinnamon over a low heat until their fragrance is released.

2 Allow the spices to cool, then transfer to a spice grinder and blitz to a fine powder. (This spice powder can be stored in a clean, dry jar for up to two months.)

3 To make the chai, combine 1 litre (1¾ pints) of water with 1 teaspoon of the spice powder in a saucepan and bring to a rapid boil. Add the tea leaves, remove from the heat.

4 Cover the tea with a lid and allow it to steep for 2–3 minutes. Strain into 4 cups and serve hot.

FIVE-SPICE MIXTURE IS PRIMARILY USED IN CHINESE CUISINE, AND ALSO IN SOME ASIAN AND ARABIC DISHES. EXTREMELY AROMATIC, IT LENDS A PUNGENT, LIQUORICE FLAVOUR TO FOOD. SOMETIMES I ADD ORANGE PEEL TO THE TEA, JUST BEFORE SERVING, TO GIVE IT ANOTHER TASTE DIMENSION.

BUTTER TEA WITH FENNEL

Serves **6** Takes **20 mins**

Ingredients

3 tbsp black tea leaves

1 tbsp fennel seeds

240ml (8fl oz) full-fat milk

salt, to taste

225g (8oz) unsalted butter

Method

1 Boil 1.5 litres (2¾ pints) of water in a saucepan. Add the tea leaves and fennel seeds and bring to the boil again. Reduce the heat and let the tea simmer for about 12–15 minutes, stirring occasionally to enhance its flavours

2 Add the milk and bring to the boil again. Remove from the heat and leave to rest for 2 minutes to allow the flavours to steep.

3 Strain the tea into a large container with a tight lid, add the salt and butter, and mix well. Alternatively, use a blender to ensure the butter is absorbed into the tea. Pour into 6 cups and serve hot.

THIS TEA BRINGS BACK MEMORIES OF MY TRIP TO BHUTAN AND TIBET, WHERE A CUP OF BUTTER TEA IS THE EPITOME OF HOSPITALITY. THE LOCALS MADE SURE THAT MY CUP WAS NEVER EMPTY. ADDING THE FENNEL SEEDS IMBUES THE TEA WITH A LIQUORICE FLAVOUR.

TRADITION WITH A TWIST

POMEGRANATE SANGRIA

Serves **4** Takes **5 mins, plus chilling**

Ingredients

480ml (16fl oz) pomegranate juice

120ml (4fl oz) cranberry juice

200g (7oz) diced mixed fruits

1 tbsp caster sugar

juice of 2 lemons

crushed ice, as required

8–10 mint leaves, to garnish

Method

1 In a large jug, combine the pomegranate juice, cranberry juice, diced fruits, sugar, and lemon juice. Stir until well mixed.

2 Cover and refrigerate until chilled. Serve over crushed ice, garnished with the mint leaves.

THIS DRINK, WITH ITS DOUBLE TREAT OF FRUITY FLAVOURS AND VIBRANT RED COLOUR, COMBINES THE HEALTH BENEFITS OF POMEGRANATE AND CRANBERRY. FOR A MIXED FRUIT SANGRIA, I PREFER TO USE PINEAPPLES, APPLES, PEACHES, PEARS, AND APRICOTS, AS THEY LEND A NICE TEXTURE AND COLOUR.

ORANGE BLOSSOM PEARTINI

Serves **4** Takes **5 mins, plus chilling**

Ingredients

480ml (16fl oz) pear juice

120ml (4fl oz) coconut water

1 tsp caster sugar

1 tsp orange blossom water

juice of 2 limes, or to taste

1 pear, vertically sliced,
to garnish

Method

1 Mix the pear juice, coconut water, sugar, orange blossom water, and lime juice in a cocktail shaker. Shake until well combined.

2 Cover and leave in the fridge to chill. Pour into 4 glasses and serve garnished with the pear slices.

YOU COULD MAKE THIS WELCOMING DRINK IN ADVANCE TO START YOUR EVENING WITH THE PERFECT COMBINATION OF SWEET, DELICATE PEAR JUICE AND CITRUSY, FLORAL ORANGE BLOSSOM.

SUGAR HILL

Serves **6** Takes **10 mins, plus chilling**

Ingredients

6 tbsp hot pink sparkling sugar crystals (if unavailable, use caster sugar)

480ml (16fl oz) tomato juice

1 tsp Tabasco sauce, or to taste

120ml (4fl oz) aloe vera juice

1 tsp honey (optional)

pinch of caster sugar

Method

1 Place the sugar crystals in a shallow dish. Moisten the rim of each glass with water and dip it into the sugar to coat it.

2 In a jug, combine the tomato juice, Tabasco, aloe vera juice, honey (if using), and caster sugar. Stir to mix well.

3 Cover and refrigerate until chilled. Pour the drink carefully into the 6 sugar-rimmed glasses and serve.

TOMATO JUICE IS A CLASSIC DRINK INGREDIENT, WHILE ALOE VERA IS WELL KNOWN FOR ITS HEALTH BENEFITS; ADDING A LITTLE HONEY OFFSETS ITS SLIGHTLY BITTER TASTE. HOT-PINK SUGAR CRYSTALS GIVE EACH FILLED GLASS AN EXTRA POP OF COLOUR.

NEW YORK DELIGHT

Serves **4** Takes **5 mins**

Ingredients

720ml (1¼ pints) fresh sugar cane juice (if unavailable, use ready-made sugar cane juice)

120ml (4fl oz) canned tomato juice

120ml (4fl oz) canned orange juice

½ tsp chilli powder

ice cubes (optional)

Method

1 Combine the sugar cane juice, tomato juice, orange juice, and chilli powder in a cocktail shaker. Add the ice cubes (if using) and shake the mixture well.

2 Divide equally between 4 glasses and serve immediately.

DURING MY CHILDHOOD, IT WAS A TREAT TO WATCH STREET HAWKERS TURN THEIR WHEELS TO EXTRACT FRESH SUGAR CANE JUICE. SERVED IN TALL GLASSES, THE JUICE HAD A REFRESHING, GRASSY SWEETNESS. YEARS LATER IN NEW YORK, I REDISCOVERED ITS TASTE AND MADE IT A BASE FOR MANY A HYDRATING RECIPE.

GRAPE COLADA

Serves **4** Takes **5 mins**

Ingredients

200g (7oz) seedless red grapes, plus 4 extra, halved, to garnish

2 tbsp honey

480ml (16fl oz) sweetened coconut cream

1 tsp cumin powder

a few drops of orange blossom water

100g (3½ oz) ice cubes

Method

1 Using a blender, blitz the grapes with honey, coconut cream, cumin powder, orange blossom water, and ice until smooth.

2 Divide the grape–coconut mixture equally between 4 glasses. Garnish with the grape halves and serve immediately.

IN THIS INTERESTING VARIATION OF A PIÑA COLADA, RED GRAPES COMBINE WELL WITH COCONUT CREAM, WHILE THE EARTHY TASTE OF CUMIN ADDS A SUBTLE SPICINESS.

GINGER–HONEY ALE

Serves **4** Takes **10 mins, plus cooling**

Ingredients

10cm (4in) fresh root ginger, sliced

3 tbsp honey

pinch of salt

juice of 2 lemons

ice cubes, as required

soda water, as required

Method

1 In a small saucepan, combine the ginger with 240ml (8fl oz) of water and bring to the boil over a medium–high heat. Cook for another 2–3 minutes until the liquid reduces by half.

2 Remove from the heat and strain into a bowl. Allow to cool before mixing in the honey, salt, and lemon juice. This concentrate can be stored in the fridge, in a clean bottle or jar, for over a week.

3 To serve, divide the ginger–honey concentrate equally between 4 glasses, top up with ice cubes and soda water, and serve.

GINGER IS SO VERSATILE THAT IT CAN BE USED IN EVERY COURSE OF A MEAL – FROM APPETIZERS AND DRINKS TO THE MAIN COURSE AND DESSERTS. IN THIS DRINK, THE PUNGENT FLAVOUR OF GINGER WORKS WELL WITH HONEY, SALT, AND LEMON TO CREATE A SOOTHING DRINK.

NOT-SO-VIRGIN MARY

Serves **4** Takes **20 mins, plus cooling and chilling**

Ingredients

6–8 medium tomatoes

1 tbsp red chilli powder

2 garlic cloves

½ tsp sea salt, plus extra for coating the rims of glasses

1 tsp cumin seeds, lightly toasted

Method

1 In a large saucepan, bring 960ml (1¾ pints) of water to a rapid boil over a medium heat. Score the base of each tomato with a cross shape using a sharp knife and add to the boiling water.

2 Boil the tomatoes for 5–7 minutes until tender. Remove from the heat and allow to cool to room temperature.

3 In a blender, blitz the cooked tomatoes and their cooking water with the red chilli powder, garlic, and sea salt to a smooth purée. Strain and refrigerate the purée until chilled.

4 To serve, moisten the rims of 4 glasses with water. Place the extra sea salt in a shallow dish and dip the rim of each glass into it to coat it. To serve, carefully pour the drink into the glasses and garnish with a sprinkle of the cumin seeds.

I LOVE THE PUNGENT TASTE OF GARLIC AND THE FIERY HEAT FROM THE RED CHILLI IN THIS DRINK. SWEET-SOUR HOME-MADE TOMATO JUICE IS PREFERABLE TO THE SHOP-BOUGHT VERSION, AS YOU WILL HAVE MORE CONTROL OVER ITS TASTE AND CONSISTENCY.

MINT JULEP MOCKTAIL

Serves **4** Takes **10 mins, plus chilling**

Ingredients

4 tbsp black tea leaves

8–10 peppermint leaves

3 tbsp honey, or to taste

juice of 3 lemons, or to taste

8–10 fresh mint leaves

400g (14 oz) crushed ice

Method

1 In a saucepan, bring 720ml (1¼ pints) of water to a rapid boil. Add the black tea leaves and peppermint leaves.

2 Remove from the heat, cover, and allow the tea to steep for 2–3 minutes. Strain, cover, and refrigerate until chilled.

3 Transfer the tea into a jug and add the honey, lemon juice, mint leaves, and crushed ice. Stir well, pour into 4 glasses, and serve.

PEPPERMINT IS THE KEY TO THIS ALCOHOL-FREE VARIATION OF CLASSIC MINT JULEP. ITS COOLING FLAVOUR MIXES WELL WITH TEA, HONEY, AND LEMON JUICE TO MAKE A COMFORTING DRINK. ADD PLENTY OF ICE TO FULLY ENJOY ITS CRISP AND INVIGORATING TASTE AND AROMAS.

PASSION FRUIT AND MACE MARTINI

Serves **4** Takes **20 mins, plus cooling**

Ingredients

1 blade dried mace

4 tbsp sugar

4 passion fruit

ice cubes, as required

Method

1 Use a mortar and pestle to grind the dried mace and sugar together to a fine powder.

2 In a saucepan, combine the sweetened mace powder with 360ml (12fl oz) of water and bring to the boil. Cut the passion fruit in half and scoop out the pulp. Add the pulp to the saucepan and cook for 2–3 minutes until the sugar dissolves and the flavours mingle.

3 Remove from the heat and allow to cool to room temperature.

4 Add some ice cubes to 4 glasses, pour the drink over the ice, and serve immediately.

THE WARM, AROMATIC, AND NUTTY FLAVOUR OF MACE COMBINES WELL WITH THE SWEET-SOUR PASSION FRUIT, CREATING A HEAVENLY TASTE OF THE TROPICS.

TECHNIQUES

Blend, muddle, and shake your way to master the drink recipes in the book with these essential techniques.

BLITZING is a technique used to mix various ingredients together to get a desired consistency. Depending on the ingredients and quantity, you can use an electric food processor or blender, or a hand-held electric blender.

MUDDLING is a method in which ingredients are pressed down and twisted with a – usually wooden – drinks mixer to release their juicy flavours before adding them to a recipe. Do not include ice while using this technique.

JUICING is a technique to extract the liquid and nutrients from fruits and vegetables, leaving behind only the fibre.

ZESTING is a method used to peel the outer layer of the skin of an orange or a lemon for flavouring desserts and drinks. Use a zester or vegetable peeler to remove zest.

CHIFFONADING is a chopping technique to cut fresh herbs and leafy vegetables into uniform, curly strips for a garnish. Roll the ingredients tightly into a cigar shape and slice into fine shreds.

SHAKING is a method in which a cocktail shaker is used to mix ingredients such as juices and alcohol with ice. Shaking should not be tried with carbonated drinks.

EQUIPMENT

Keep these kitchen tools handy before you start working with any of the drink recipes.

▲ Hardwood chopping board

▲ Measuring jug

▲ Pestle and mortar

▶ Cocktail shaker

▲ Measuring spoons

◀ Glass jug

▶ Blender

▲ Peeler, corer, and zester

▲ Lemon squeezer

◀ Muddler

▲ Hand grater

▶ Sieve

▶ Hand-held blender

▲ Saucepan

▲ Ice-cream scoop

▲ Coffee grinder

171

INDEX

For DK UK
Angliciser and editor Susannah Steel
Senior editor Kathryn Meeker
Senior art editor Glenda Fisher
Editor Alice Kewellhampton
Additional photography Charlotte Tolhurst
Additional food styling Kate Wesson
Index Vanessa Bird
Pre-production producer Robert Dunn
Producer Stephanie McConnell
Creative technical support Sonia Charbonnier
Managing editor Stephanie Farrow
Managing art editor Christine Keilty

For DK India
Editors Medha Gupta, Hina Jain
Designers Sukriti Sobti, Devika Awasthi, Astha Singh
Illustrators Sukriti Sobti, Devika Awasthi, Arun Pottirayil
Photographers Vikas Khanna, Dayakar Soma
Food stylist Parul Pratap Shirazi
Proofreaders Dipali Singh, Alka Thakur
Jacket designers Shefali Upadhyay, Sukriti Sobti
Picture researcher Nishwan Rasool
Picture research manager Taiyaba Khatoon
Managing editor Alka Ranjan
Design consultant Shefali Upadhyay
DTP designers Nandkishor Acharya, Shanker Prasad
Production manager Pankaj Sharma
DTP manager Balwant Singh
Managing director, India Aparna Sharma

First published in Great Britain in 2017 by
Dorling Kindersley Limited
80 Strand, London, WC2R 0RL

A WORLD OF IDEAS:
SEE ALL THERE IS TO KNOW
www.dk.com

ACKNOWLEDGMENTS

**The publisher would like to thank the following for their
kind permission to reproduce their photographs:**

(Key: b-below/bottom; c-centre; l-left)
**16, 23, 24, 27, 31, 32, 34, 38, 41, 43, 44, 47, 53, 55, 59, 67, 79,
93, 94, 97, 108, 111, 113, 119, 127, 130, 135, 137, 140, 142, 149, 166,
169 Vikas Khanna. 171 Dorling Kindersley: Ian O'Leary (clb)**

All other images © Dorling Kindersley

For further information see: www.dkimages.com